How to win an argument
Even when you're wrong

The 9 laws of debate

Dr William P Helpington

Dedication

To my ex-wife, who took all of my good stuff and got it on with the neighbor. Go fuck yourself!

Table of Contents

Introduction

What I'm going to give you is the tools that experts don't want you to have.

While other masters of the practice of argument and debate seem to want to keep a level of integrity, I don't give a shit about that because this is not about making friends, it's about winning.

Now let's define that for a moment because some people might say that convincing someone of your side of the argument requires a level of decorum so to win over the person you're arguing with. This is bullshit. The fact that they are arguing means they've already made up their mind. **The only people you need to convince are the onlookers**.

I like the example of Indiana Jones. He is one of our most beloved action heroes, but he's also one hell of a dirty fighter. That is in spite of his likability, it's actually part of it. He's always an underdog in the fights he gets into but does whatever it takes to win. People love that. This is the reason that I enjoy arguing a seemingly unwinnable argument.

Why would you want to argue when you know you're wrong? Because it's fun! It's a step beyond devil's advocate into a realm where you are making people think. The idea of "steel-manning" is something quite fascinating to me.

The idea is that you take a position contrary to your own and try to argue it as if you do believe it. This is in stark contrast to what people often do which is straw-manning. I would advise against the strawman type arguments when possible, but in the last section I'll cover some of the more devious tactics you can pull out when all else fails.

Now go forth and annoy...

Chapter 1: The law of preparation

The law of preparation

If you are planning to argue with or debate someone you have to have respect for them. At the very least you must have respect for their ability to argue. I mainly say this because nothing feels worse than coming out of a conflict that you went into ill-prepared.

Know everything you can about your opponent when possible; certainly, where it comes to matters of relevance.

In "How to Hitler" I wrote bout the power of transforming issues either from moral to logical, or vice versa – while that book is certainly meant to be tongue in cheek, but it is actually pretty effective when trying to win. The idea is that when trying to win in the eyes of the observers, you can do it on one of three ways...

1. they like your logic
2. they like your virtue
3. they like YOU!

If you are prepared with facts and data to support your position you can often win on the logic side of it, but morality tends to trump logic. For example, one can make a pretty sound argument for eugenics in the interest of evolving the human race, and yet it's pretty morally reprehensible. So how do we overcome this?

By ourselves claiming the moral high ground. You can either do this by making use of previous information you have on your opponent, or by using generalizations about people who fall into their umbrella, for example, desperate Dan wants to convince his homophobic counterpart that eugenics is optimal...

> Desperate Dan: Shouldn't we do everything in our power to make sure children aren't born with diseases, disabilities or homosexuality.

Not only did Dan appeal morally to the person he was speaking directly to, but by beginning talking about disease and disability appealed to a much broader range and will more likely win over his viewers. That of course was a personal appeal, but he could easily leave out the homosexual comment and make it a winnable point for many people.

The bottom line is that the more you know in advance, both about your subject and the person you will be debating, the better off you will be.

Chapter 2: The law of interviewing

The law of interviewing

There are a lot of ways to win debates, but the first thing you always want to do when possible, is rather counter-intuitive, which is: ask, don't tell.

Preparation for a good debate is vital, and you certainly have a lot you want to say, but instead look for opportunities to **ask them questions**. This is especially useful when you can put one of your points into the question.

The beauty of being in interviewer or question mode, is that you subtly place all of the responsibility onto their shoulders – it is now their burden to convince you.

Questions of course have many forms. I've always enjoyed questions that begin with "how" because they are a powerful transference of responsibility.

Leading, or loaded questions are generally not advised because they can make you look bad, but in a pinch they can help which is why I've included them in the last chapter.

There's not much else to say about this, but it comes up a lot in the chapters to come, so cement it into your mind: **whenever possible switch into question mode by asking questions**.

Chapter 3: The law of likeability

The law of Likability

Remembering that arguments are won in one of three ways...
1. they like your logic
2. they like your virtue
3. they like YOU!

...Let's assume for a moment that they don't follow your logic or even your morals. All you have to work with at that point is making people like you.

The first and easiest thing you can do is smile - not a creepy, forced smile, but that smile that says "this is fun". This sways people in a sneaky way. It not only tells them you are a fun person, but suggests that you might be screwing with the other guy and they want to enjoy the ride with you.

Another way to become likeable is to say back to the other party what they've said in question form, but not just any old question, like what they've said is utterly absurd.

Let's take an example where Mike wants to convince Stupid Sam of something slightly morally wrong, without much evidence to support his theory.

> Stupid Sam: any group or organization that victimizes people is immoral.

> Mike: victimizing people is immoral?

Stupid Sam: of course it is.

Mike: but stealing isn't always wrong.

Stupid Sam: that depends on what you mean by stealing.

Mike: what I mean by stealing? Isn't it pretty obvious?

Stupid Sam: if you're talking about forcefully taking someone else's possessions, then yes.

Mike (smiling): so by your logic, any government that has ever taken taxes is immoral?

Stupid Sam: taxes is different from stealing.

Mike: but these entities you suggest are immoral give people the option of opting out if they choose, governments don't.

Stupid Sam: suck my balls!

Mike has used his charm and wit to put Stupid Sam on the defensive, for a position that is completely irrational. Mike has also used the interviewer technique quite nicely, leading Sam with questions.

Another way to win the likability game is to appear as more of a moderate than your opponent.

It may well be that what they are saying is perfectly reasonable, but to win over the audience you should come across as the one closer to the centerline and push them towards the extreme. This is easiest to demonstrate with an example. Pete is talking the more "extreme" position of climate change denial… now not many of these people actually exist, more commonly what happens is that people are accused of being "deniers" when in fact what they are against is the proposed solutions, but for the sake of this example I'm going to pretend that Pete actually wants to disprove his chum Tad on the idea.

> Pete: climate change isn't even proven. It's only about virtue politics.

> Tad: what are you talking about? There's tons of evidence.

> Pete: there's evidence of fluctuating weather, but that has been happening since the ice age and they've only begun measuring it in the last few years. And now these politicians want us to feel so guilty about driving to work to pay THEIR salaries, that we buy into their tax scheme – which by the way is a completely insane, not to mention unproven way to address the issue.

Tad: well, we've got to do something.
Pete: why do we?

Tad: because sitting back and doing
nothing isn't going to help.

Pete: then why not start banging your
head on a wall, it will have just about as
much impact – and without the tax you'll
actually be able to afford the medical
costs.

Tad: the tax will be barely noticeable to
you and me, it's the big polluting
companies that will feel it most and be
incentivized to look for better options.

Pete: a few problems with that... to say
that we won't feel it and only big
companies will is crazy. What do you think
these companies will do when their profits
decrease, just take it? Of course not,
they'll pass their costs onto consumers
and essentially raise inflation, giving us
less money to spend on the more
expensive gas we need. If these guys really
wanted to incentivize them they'd give
benefits for using renewable energy, not
charging them money at gunpoint.

Tad: it's not at "gun point".

Pete: you're right, it's worse than that
because you're forcing them to pay more

without any choice in the matter; it's classic totalitarianism.

Tad: Fuck you!

Pete, sort of changed the subject here from climate change to the proposed carbon tax. This was wise because he knew that on the merits of climate change he was not likely to win many supporters, but he could push himself more towards the moderate by taking issue with the proposed solution. And then after discrediting the concept with an example that wasn't very scientific, it was more hypothetical – but it showed he put thought into it. Finally, he brilliantly concluded it by suggesting that the idea was "totalitarianism" which of course is extremely extreme.

In order to know where the happy medium of society is you sort of need to keep your finger on the pulse of trends so that you can appear as moderate as possible when arguing.

As an aside, Tad also utilized a technique that I haven't talked much about because I don't feel like it, but it is certainly worth noting... one of the best ways to play with people's emotions is via story-telling. Think about it, this is something that our race has been doing since the beginning of time. Films do it. Telling a story – even one that's not true – can connect to your audience in a very powerful way, so whenever possible, come up with one or two stories that support your point.

Humility is another way to come across as
likable. You are probably not going to argue your
way out of a parking ticket, but you very well
might charm your way out of one by being
humble.

Chapter 4: the law of proof

The law of Proof

One of the first things to do is place the burden of proof on the other party, that is well known, but to squeeze the most out of this you must place it on them when it rightfully belongs on you.

One of my favourite examples of this is the God argument. Now if there is a debate about the existence of God, one would think that the burden of proof is on the one trying to convince others that there IS a God. So, let's see how "Mike" masterfully tricks "Stupid Sam" into having to prove otherwise.

Stupid Sam: moderate religious people provide a cover for the extremists.

Mike: how is that different than you using the extremists to justify your hatred for the moderates?

Stupid Sam: I don't hate the moderates I hate the religion.

Mike: then why do you insult them at every opportunity, as if you suggest they are mentally inferior to you?

Stupid Sam: because they have chosen to believe in something that is as logical as believing in the Easter Bunny.

Mike: and why do you suppose they do that?

Stupid Sam: because they either don't know any better or have been manipulated by religious leaders.

Mike: and how do your followers know that you didn't use these same manipulation techniques to persuade them?

Stupid Sam: because what I say can be demonstrated by scientific methods.

Mike: okay then, use the scientific method right now to prove the lack of a deity.

Stupid Sam: no. Up yours!

See what Mike has done? By being on the asking end of things he makes the other side come up with the answers. Slowly he has led Stupid Sam down a path that leads to the ultimate switch. He does this by first making Stupid Sam defend his character and calling into question his motives. Most importantly, he accused him of *hypocrisy*, accusing him of doing exactly what he is arguing against. Mike does this a couple of times within this exchange. It can't be understated how powerful this is, as we will cover in chapter 6.

Chapter 5: The law of time control

The law of Time control

Time is a huge factor in any debate and coming up with good responses is only part of the battle, you also have to come up with your good responses FAST!

There are a few ways to give the illusion of this as well as some tricks to speed up your responses.

The first and easiest thing to do is to give yourself additional time by asking your opponent to clarify something even if you know exactly what they are talking about. This buys you a little more time to construct your rebuttal.

While it is always a good idea to come prepared with your arguments, be careful not to say what you want to say when the time isn't right, or it doesn't flow naturally.

You can also manipulate time by confusing the hell out of your opponent. Better still is to only *slightly* confuse them, that way they take a moment or two longer to react. The quickest way to do that is to mess with your sentence structure. Say your point slightly different than you would normally do it.

Instead of "Hormones in milk can cause cancer."

Try saying "Cancer can be caused by the hormones in milk."

This not only makes them think back to the beginning of your sentence to remember what your point is, but it also slightly changes what is most readily in their mind. So if there is something you are trying to sneak past them, hiding it at the beginning of a sentence can work wonders – although that is not the point I'm trying to make here.

Time seems to slow down internally, and stress can build up which makes a pause feel longer than it is, while your brain is not functioning well. Try this – next time you are stumped say "hmm, that's interesting." That kind of laid back, casual response buys you time to think while also freeing your brain of stress.

Take a nice long deep breath if you start to feel a little stressed. The oxygen will do you good. Rephrase the question or statement both out loud and internally as much as you need to sort through it.

When in doubt, don't be afraid to admit when you don't know something. If someone cites an obscure study or a fact you've never heard, let them know and even try to downplay its importance and/or relevance. Or even better still, ask for specific details about it, chances are they don't have that information and they will be the ones to look like a fool.

Chapter 6: The law of making them a hypocrite

The law of making them a hypocrite

Discrediting your opponent is always handy, but if you can demonstrate that their logic is in contradiction with itself, you are on your way to not only winning, but making them look foolish – which is really fun.

The way in which we want to do this is by having THEM come to the conclusion that they are being inconsistent. Sometimes they see what you're doing and have no other choice but to try to cleverly duck and roll – but don't let them off the hook.

Doing this however often means getting a little background information on your opponent, such as Mike does to Stupid Sam here. I know I'm picking on poor Sam, but he deserves it.

> Stupid Sam: Religion is stupid because they don't have any evidence for their claims.
>
> Mike: Is evidence really important for you?
>
> Stupid Sam: It's the ONLY thing important to me.
>
> Mike: Interesting. So when the judge was being accused of sexual misconduct when there was absolutely no corroborating evidence, and the only other testimonies were contrary – why were you tweeting out that everyone should unquestioningly believe the accusations?

In this case Stupid Sam set himself up for this
with a series of poorly conceived twitters. But
when this isn't available we have to look for
contradictions within the argument itself.

Let's look at another situation, Julie is trying to
convince Lance that a universal income would
solve poverty, but Lance is having none of it.
Watch how each side tries to discredit the
other…

> Julie: If we really care about ending
> poverty we need to try something different.
> A universal income would lift up people
> who can't help themselves.

> Lance: In that type of system who would
> determine what the poverty line is?

> Julie: There would have to be a committee
> to do various calculations and determine
> what it is.

> Lance: And how will the government make
> sure that this price doesn't change so
> quickly that the people sink right back
> into poverty?

> Julie: by putting restrictions on what
> people can charge.

> Lance: and when it becomes unprofitable
> for companies to own land, make goods or
> perform services, how will the government
> deal with the housing, goods and services
> shortage?

Julie: It never would. Inflation would be controlled.

Lance: Because the top one percent who can afford it most will be taxed higher, right?

Julie: yes, but they are not good at sharing their wealth anyway.

Lance: I agree. They didn't get rich by giving away more than they have to. So once you raise taxes on these greedy people, what is there incentive to not lay people off, cut benefits or even relocate to maintain their profit margins?

Julie: the government won't let them.

Lance: that sounds like a lot is dictated by this government. Is that what you really want, an all-powerful dictatorship?

This is full of great examples. Lance has wisely chosen to begin with questions and make Julie prove her point. However, in the process he guides her towards the conclusion that wealth people are greedy. He even disarms her with an agreement, then sticks it to her by showing why her presupposition causes a detrimental problem to what she is arguing for.

Now the truth with this is that no one likes to be made into a hypocrite, so while it may win you points on the debate front it may lose you friends in process, so use with caution.

Chapter 7: The law of context

The law of context

In every argument there are two things at play: content and context.

The content is the words used where as the context is how the words are used. The context is what the argument is really about.

The content can be deciphered from the context, but the reverse is not necessarily true.

This probably sounds obscure, so here's an example: let's say we are having a debate about abortion… the context of this is everything because the pro-choice position makes the context about women's rights, ergo if you disagree you hate women. Conversely, the pro-life makes it about the sanctity of indefensible life. Ergo if you disagree you think it's okay to kill helpless babies. While the overall content is about "abortion" the context is so vastly different that these two sides will never agree.

So how can we use this to win an argument?

The first step is to recognize their context and then debunk it.

In the above case, if Liberal Larry was arguing for "women's rights" and Conservative Cameron was on the other side trying to convince him, it might look like this.

> Conservative Cameron: If women's rights
> are so important to you, why wouldn't you
> want to protect female fetuses as well?
>
> Liberal Larry: because you touch yourself
> at night!

See how Cameron completely threw Larry? Now
let's try the other way.

> Liberal Larry: if defending fetus rights are
> so important to you, why are you also
> okay with oppressing gays?
>
> Conservative Cameron: because gays are
> weird.

This trick of context gets two sides on the same
page but can also get people arguing about
things they never were in the first place. In the
two examples above they acknowledged the
other side's context which says "we're arguing
the same thing", but then threw in a twist that
had the opponent arguing a different case.
Cameron's argument works slightly better
because it is changing the context from Larry's
point to his own, where as the example of Larry
had him switching the context from Cameron's
point to a different time me of Cameron's points
that seems contradictory. While this can
sometimes discredit your opposition, you have to
be careful with it because it may open the door
or to the other side getting to validate a second
one of their own views and solidify their
character in a way you hadn't anticipated.

Speaking of gays, what about the subject of gay marriage? Curiously this is still a point of contention. So how would one take up the unpopular position of opposing it while winning over the audience?

Liberal Larry: if you can get married, why shouldn't homosexuals be allowed to?

Conservative Cameron: this isn't about me, it's about a child's right to have a mother and a father.

Liberal Larry: just because someone is straight doesn't make them a good parent.

Conservative Cameron: maybe not but the model has worked for the entirety of our species' existence.

Liberal Larry: and do we want to teach our children that being born gay makes you inferior?

Conservative Cameron: why would you teach them something homophobic like that?

Liberal Larry: not me, that's what you're doing.

Conservative Cameron: I find it weird that the only way you can think of taking care of children involves being cruel to homosexuals. They don't deserve that.

Liberal Larry: Stop trying to turn this around on me. I'm the one fighting for their rights.

Conservative Cameron: I'm sorry you're so angry that I called out your phony gesture for the intolerance it really is, I just don't think that just anyone should be able to go get a licence to get children. Maybe you think it's okay for pedophiles to do so, but I don't.

Liberal Larry: Fuck you!

Once again Cameron turned Larry's argument on its head by using his own accusation against him. This began by changing the context of the argument away from the notion of free love to the context of protecting the innocent.

Chapter 8: The law of confusion

The law of confusion

Ever seen Karate Kid 3? Me either, but the evil Sendai in that teaches the kid of three laws which are kind of devious but unquestionably true: if your enemy can't stand he can't fight, if he can't breathe, he can't fight, and if he can't see he can't fight. Sexist, but you get my point.

The law of confusion is about confusion is sort of like the rhetoric version of this. You are throwing them off balance by obscuring their senses.

I will teach you how to use this against other, how to defend against it and how to counter-strike.

The best way to begin saying something confusing is to take an obscure examples or statistics from somewhere they are not likely to be able to validate in the moment. The beauty of stats is that they can be easily manipulated by excluding information. So let's take a debate about gun control. You can take the a study that compares the US, Canada and Mexico and swing it any way you like. Here are the approximate numbers from 2011 - of course you can use any year you like.

Canada (heavy gun control):
Total Murders: 600
Murders by firearm: 180 (30%)

USA (moderate gun control):

Total Murders: 25,000
Murders by firearm: 10,000 (40%)

Mexico (what even is gun control?):
Total Murders: 37,000
Murders by firearm: 11,000 (29%)

So at a quick glance you might be able to see how you can manipulate this data:

For gun control: the stricter the gun control, the fewer the gun-related murders.

Against: the stricter the gun control, the higher percentage of gun-related murders (discounting Canada because - well everyone does).

The more obscure the study or reference the better, just come up with something that has a grain of truth and sounds credible and you're golden.

Otherwise useless facts are fantastic because your opponent will almost inevitably be caught off-guard. Here's an example.

> Stupid Sam: Religion is foolish because there is no evidence for it.

> Mike: who defines what "evidence" means?

> Stupid Sam: the scientific community.

Mike: the same community who, like yourself has a vested interest in withholding contradictory evidence?

Stupid Sam: Scientist don't do that, religions do.

Mike: I take it you are familiar with the concept of data dredging, the French scientists for example, who withheld vital information about the pyramids.

Stupid Sam: People make mistakes, that doesn't make all of science wrong.

Mike: But how do you know who to put your trust in? Surely you didn't go into outer space and see the Earth for yourself to determine it was round, so who has earned your faith.

Stupid Sam: people with rational explanations.

Mike: you mean people whose explanations corroborate and make sense with your pre-existing, subjective way of reasoning.

Stupid Sam: I suppose so.

Mike: But your subjective thinking can't be demonstrated outside of your own mind. Even less demonstrable is your emotional and moral logic. So why is your internal method more valid than someone else's?

Stupid Sam: Because you're fat!

Once again Mike tripped up Stupid Sam H. In this case he used Sam's arrogance against him and by throwing in the example of the pyramids, ever so subtly to make his point, thus force-fed his mind just enough extra to get him off his game.

Another way to confuse is by the unnecessary use of complex language. Words that work well in a debate are "lawyer" words like: Conflating, corroborative, copious, irrefutable, reprehensible, deposition, unavailing, moratory, boondoggle, Circumlocution etc.

Defending against it is surprisingly easy, you just have to be aware of it. If someone says something that sounds overly complex or confusing, simply say something along the lines of these:

> Retort 1: are you trying to make a point?
> Retort 2: I have no idea what you're talking about and I suspect you don't either.
> Retort 3: you're not very good at speaking in human are you?
> Retort 4: can you say that in a way that is sensible?

Retort 5: I haven't read that study, I've been too busy living in the real world...

The beauty of this is that you are not only forcing them to speak plainly while also winning over audience approval. Now what if you have used the confusion tactic and they have turned it on you? This is when you counter strike with:

Counter-strike 1: no problem, I'll do my best to speak in single-syllables for you.
Counter-strike 2: I apologize, I was led to believe I would be debating someone who is educated.
Counter-strike 3: No.
Counter-strike 4: sure, what speed would you like me to slow down to?

Chapter 9: The law of frustration

The law of frustration

This is all about making them WANT to quit out of exasperation. This is methodical, and the approach is to "castrate" their tactics, undermine their reasoning and call their character into question. Remember in the beginning we talked about the three ways that debates are won? Well they are lost by the same things. To refresh your memory, they are:

1. character
2. logic
3. compassion

These three areas were identified by the ancient Greek philosophers and rhetoricians as: ethos, logos and pathos. But who gives a shit about that, let's figure out how to dismantle and destroy your opponent.

It is best to begin with their logic, because it is slightly detached from them and does not make you look like the bully you really are. With their logic in question, we can then go after their call their motives into question which calls into question their character and sways the emotions of the audience to you for being the hero who is unveiling this.

Since I've picked on Liberal Larry a couple of times already, I am going to keep it fair here by picking on him again. Just for a laugh let's do

the endlessly hilarious debate of Trump's wall.
This time I will interrupt the exchange from time
to time to point out what is happening.

> Liberal Larry: In order to be the kind of
> people we need we have welcome people of
> all ethnicities, not keep out anyone who is
> brown.

What Larry has done here, is to suggest that if
you don't take his side, you are a racist. But in
reality, that has nothing to do with the argument
at hand. If Cameron tries to deny the allegation
he has actually given more weight to the
accusation. Instead he has to nip it in the bud.
An effective way to do so, is to call it for what it
is, a baseless accusation of a desperate person.

> Conservative Cameron: I thought we were
> here to have an honest discussion about
> the pros and cons of a border wall, can we
> talk about that or are we just going to sit
> here and throw despicable accusations
> back and forth, because we could do that
> if you'd rather.

> Liberal Larry: My point is that the strength
> of our society is in its diversity.

> Conservative Cameron: I appreciate you
> sharing that without the disparaging
> remarks, can I ask you a question about
> your position?

Liberal Larry: of course, that's what we're here for.

Conservative Cameron: Is your opposition to the wall out of fear that it will work, or out of fear that it won't?

Boom. In one fell swoop, Cameron kicked the legs out from under his opponent. First of all, he doubled down on the character charge, reminding the audience to be on the lookout for such attacks, then moved into question mode. The specific question is sort of a false dilemma, meaning he has given two options which are not necessarily the only possible choices. Maybe Larry's opposition to the wall is something totally different, maybe he thinks it will look ugly. Who knows? But posing the question this way paints him into a corner. Adding to this the fact that he specifically suggested it was fear driving his opponent's thought process makes him look weak, not the kind of person anyone respects. Now let's help poor Larry get things on track.

Liberal Larry: The only thing I fear is people like you trying to make the situation worse for people who are already desperate. Why would anyone do that to another human being?

Larry has subtly inserted yet another character attack while ducking the actual question. He's also switched into question mode himself. The best thing Cameron can do in this case is trying to ignore the character attacks and ignore the question to move the discussion back to where he wants it.

> Conservative Cameron: so, can I take that to mean that your greater fear is that it WILL work?

At this point in the debate, both sides are well aware of what is going on. Each one is trying to get into interviewer mode. An attempt on Larry's side to continue this will only serve to annoy the opposition, so instead he will make a statement that simultaneously makes his point while attacking his opponent's logic. He is careful not to attack his character seeing as this tactic has already been called out.

> Liberal Larry: I think that what the world needs is more compassion and less hatred. THAT'S why I don't want a wall.

> Conservative Cameron: Because of compassion?

> Liberal Larry: Yes. Compassion for everyone!

Larry has done a clever thing here by once again calling ethics into the debate. He suggests that what he is after is the only compassionate option. It's also something of a false dilemma. Cameron has rebottled with the mirror technique, skeptically restating the virtue Larry seems to be after. This is also a bit of a slight on his character because it is subtly calling him a liar. Larry doubles down, making sure to use the word "everyone" because it implies that Cameron is racially motivated. Cameron decides to further discredit Larry's position by the following statement which follows a very clear line of reasoning.

> Conservative Cameron: It seems to me that if your motivation is compassion you would want to protect American citizens from outside threats. WE get to decide who comes into our country.

By emphasizing the word "we", Cameron has put a unifying pronoun and accompanied it with control. This feels empowering, and feeling empowered feels good! Not heroine good, but still good. High marks indeed, but he can't sit on his butt-plug just yet, because Larry is a smart bloke. He has a few options here. He could dismantle the word "we" and redefine it to mean "you". That might work, but having made so many character attacks already it might not be the best tactic. Instead he's going to try to put the pressure back on Cameron.

> Liberal Larry: so, you would be okay with people dying because they can't get across the border?

This was a bit of a risky move by Larry, but he's desperate to discredit Cameron. Now his assertion raises all kinds of questions, which makes it difficult for Cameron to distill them into one thought.

> Conservative Cameron: this isn't what I'm okay with, this is what I'm not okay with. I'm not okay with breaking and entering and I'm not okay with crossing borders illegally.

This is a pretty solid approach. He made no secret of the fact he is changing the context, but rather made it very blunt, which has the subtext of discrediting his opponent. He has then drawn a comparison between illegal border crossing and breaking and entering. In this case he kept the word "illegal" at the very end, and this was not by chance. He could've said "illegal entry" or some other variation, but he wanted the word "illegal" to stand out in people's minds. Partly because is has a negative connotation all on its own, but also because it is the very word that his opponents like to leave out when trying to

undermine their character. Now how ought
Larry to rebuttal? Again, he has a few options.
He can try to re-frame the situation again by
saying that there is a difference between private
property and country borders, but that might
just end in a circular argument. Larry must dig
deep and pull out all of the stops. He is going to
go after Cameron's credibility by suggesting that
he is blinded by his privilege, and then make an
honest attempt to lay out his intent. This gets
extra power at this time because his hesitance to
raise this seemingly noble position early on gives
him a tone of humility, which is very character-
lifting.

> Liberal Larry: well, it must be nice for you
> to get to sit in your position of privilege
> and dictate who gets to be free and who
> doesn't, but I want to live in a world where
> we have open arms to those in need,
> where we lead the way with compassion
> and protection.
>
> Conservative Cameron: I'm sure you really
> do think that you're being noble by
> endangering your fellow countrymen. I'd
> like to see more compassion as well, but
> how can we protect other people when we
> are too busy turning a blind-eye to
> injustice to protect our own citizens from
> invasion?

Larry had him on the ropes, but Cameron did something devious here. He knocked down his opponent's claim not, by claiming he is a liar, but by claiming he is misguided. He then went after his opponent's defenses by making a slight concession, but mercilessly suggested that his opponent's means won't accomplish the ends, or at the very least, not a good version of them.

Chapter 10: Dirty debating tricks

Dirty debating tricks

So far, we've mostly kept it above the belt, but sometimes when you are trying to win a losing cause you need to role in the mud and hope you don't get caught in it.

As mentioned previously, "How to Hitler" is a better source of nasty tricks because it has nearly 150 ways to overtake people if being evil isn't a concern, but here are a few specific to arguing to think about...

Misdirection

This is the equivalent of the kid saying "hey, what's that", pointing to the sky and running away as soon as the other guy's back is turned.

There are different ways to do this whether via a strawman or other red herring. You're drawing their attention away from the actual issue (context) at hand and trying to shift the focus. This can be done by using "what about..." type arguments quite nicely. Of course, the farther you stray from the context the more likely you are to get caught in it. For example, if you're trying to make a case for the merits of veganism, don't say "well what about that study that connected vaccinating babies with autism?"

False equivalents

This is a pretty sneaky one to use, but again has to be handled with care because if you get caught in it you are likely to be made into a fool.

I love the example of my ex-niece saying, "I should get an ipad because all the other parents are getting one for their kids". This is falsely comparing the children, the parents and also throwing in a "fact" that is difficult to contest.

Tautology

Tautology is not a common phrase, but this is basically where your argument is doing the equivalent of saying "the grass is green therefore the grass is green". Now that seems stupid, but it is also stupidly obvious. If we re-word that so that it is less obvious what is being done, we get into tautology. Every argument has two components: a proposition and proof of that proposition. By basically making those two things identical you are not proving anything but still making a valid point.

Here is a less obvious example: "The temperature is constantly rising because this summer was hotter than last summer."

Using your argument against itself

This is probably a little abstract, but I'm sure you've heard politicians accusing other politicians of using fear tactics? What are they doing? They're using our fear of fear to frighten you. You can do the same with guilt, Stupid Sam did the same with demagoguery.

Ignorance as evidence

I've heard this used countless times and all it does is put an argument into the realm of unwinnable. While it's not my favourite to use, I view it as getting out of checkmate and into a stalemate. Example: "you can't disprove God exists therefore you can't be right".

The inability to prove something does not make the opposite so, but this is sort of what the ignorance tactic tries to accomplish. Like I said, it is not likely to convince anyone of anything because intuitively we know that these are somewhat nonsensical, but if used artfully can help you wriggle to safety.

Conclusion

I hope you've enjoyed this short text on winning arguments. Remember, arguing should always be fun. If you are at a point in an argument where you start thinking "jeez, I might be wrong on this one", that is not the time to step down from your position, it's the time to ramp up your use of these techniques.

And just to plug my other books one final time, the art of being a complete shit is covered very thoroughly in "How to Hitler", while "The Vegan Bible" is focussed on the foolishness specific to vegans, it can also help you begin to recognize the hypocrisy in other ideologies.